Graduating with Honors: Mastering the Police Academy

Graduating with Honors: Mastering the Police Academy

Xavier Wells

ISBN 13: 9781700522597

Publisher: CRC Publishing

Table of Contents

Introduction

et me just start off by saying congratulations to those of you finding this book after being hired on by an agency. Kudos are truly in order; not everyone makes it through the police application process. By being one of the select few chosen to attend the academy, you've displayed the character, skills, and values that your department is looking for, so you got the job. If you are finding this book earlier in your journey, then just know you'll benefit greatly; being prepared in this profession goes a long way in terms of your success in the hiring process, your success in the academy , your reputation in the department, and keeping you alive once you hit the streets.

The academy is the be-all, end-all for every police applicant during their hiring process. To receive that invitation letter is to reach the culmination of all of your hard work manifest in a single piece of paper. Make no mistake, though, to those of you still in the police hiring process, it is very demanding, and many don't make it through on the first go around; some don't ever make it. This, however, is a book about the police academy, so we won't be covering too much on the hiring process here. So, if you need help or a leg up, check out our other resource *From Applicant to Police Cadet*, available on Amazon.

So why this book? Well, there is a prevalent problem among police applicants turned prospective cadets, and that issue is mind-set. Often, an applicant will pull out all the stops during the hiring process; they'll work out, study, train, everything, just to get hired. But sustaining this performance over six to twelve months takes a toll on them mentally. Then they fall off. You see, for many applicants, the goal, the sole purpose for working hard and training harder, is to get hired by a police department. Once that's achieved, they release the proverbial big sigh: "I've made it; I can take a breather." What applicants fail to realize is that getting into the academy isn't the end, but the beginning. Everything you had to do and overcome will pale in comparison to what will be required of you at the academy. The purpose of this book is to get you mentally prepared to not only graduate the academy but do so with honors.

Honors? What honors? Yes, honors; every police academy that I know of has some type of award system to recognize outstanding performance in different areas. Areas such as firearms proficiency, defensive tactics, leadership, fitness, education, and the overall best top cadet. You won't learn to hide in the crowd in this book; here, you'll be given the best information to not only graduate but to stand out from your peers and get recognized at graduation. At the end of the day, if you're going to do something, you might as well try to be the best at it. We're going to break down the academy, what will be expected of you, and how to succeed. Remember that information changes situations. Hopefully, through this resource, many if not all of the questions, mystery, and suspense around the police academy can be answered for you, allowing you to focus on executing and excelling in your academy training.

CHAPTER 1

What Is the Academy, Really?

The Basics

As I stated earlier, just because you received that final offer of employment doesn't mean you're automatically entitled to a badge, gun, and graduation. There is going to be a lot more involved before achieving those goals than you realize. Even after your graduation from the police academy, you'll still have to make it through the FTO program to keep your job and be recognized as a full-fledged officer.

Academies also vary in every aspect from state to state, city to city, and department to department. Each state has different training requirements, laws, and procedures. Some areas in the United States require cadets to go through academies held at local community colleges or other state-sponsored institutions to earn a state certification before you can apply to a department. Others may be through actual police departments, which is often the more traditional route. No matter where you go, you'll be receiving extensive training and a flood of new information and skills. The majority of your instruction will be classroom based, but don't let that fool you. There will be plenty of opportunities for your class to receive extracurricular instruction outside, in the form of exercise (more on that later). As your academy instruction progresses, you'll also be exposed to scenarios based on real-world events. This is so when you hit the streets and take your first call, it won't be the first time you're seeing that kind of situation, and you don't freeze.

The academy is a place where future police officers are made. I'm going to need you to take that in for a second because it's powerful stuff. There is no way in hell you can become a police officer without going through someone's academy. The fact that you've been selected means you're in rarified air. There are thousands out there who wish they had the opportunity you're living right now. This is the mind-set you need to have every day you show up for training in order to be successful. This profession must be honored, your opportunity treasured. The profession is getting harder and harder every year in every way imaginable. Men and women coming in need to be trained and versed in a myriad of topics and skills. From MED TAC to pursuit and active shooter, the police academy will expose you to situations that require 100 percent of your effort and abilities.

The academy will also be a place to strip you down to the core and build you up as a law enforcement officer. Fighting that process will only make things harder on you and your classmates. You'll quickly find out that law enforcement is a paramilitary organization, meaning that there is a huge emphasis placed on rank and seniority. Typically, a police department's chain of command will start with the rank of officer or deputy, or in the case of state agencies, trooper. Other ranks will include sergeants, lieutenants, captains, majors, and commanders. Somewhere at the bottom of the ladder is the police academy recruit, which will be you. The best academy advice you'll get anywhere: shut your mouth, show respect, learn, be a team player, and do your time. They'll love you.

What will be covered in the academy?

The easy answer is obviously, everything. Of course, if I left it at that, you wouldn't have too much of a reason to continue reading this book. So . . . the full answer is a lot more complicated. As I stated before, training standards vary widely over the geographic landscape of the United States. Departments located in different regions will also have different emergencies that affect the residents of their jurisdictions. For example, a police department in Florida will have more extensive wet road driving than a police department in, say, Nevada. The last time I checked, there weren't hurricanes or tropical storms for the landlocked state of Nevada. Similarly, the police department in Florida probably doesn't do any training for blizzards or ice road hazards because it doesn't snow. Are you starting to get my point? There are, however, many basic critical competencies with being a police officer that are mirrored across all police departments in the United States.

According to the Bureau of Justice, the average academy duration ranges anywhere from twenty-one weeks to six months. That is just an average, Academies can be as long as eight to nine months in some states. I've always been of the mind-set of the longer, the better; you can never have too much training. Better trained officers mean more officers going home at the end of their shifts and better service to the community. It's a win–win situation.

The following sections will list the training and skills you'll receive when you enter the academy and how to best prepare for each.

Operations

Report Writing

If you don't like to write, you screwed yourself with this job. There won't be a day that goes by on the streets where you won't need some sort of written correspondence. Police report writing isn't like writing a college paper. There is a lot more on the line for all parties involved, and you'll be trying to gather information in a hectic and dynamic environment.

In the academy, you'll learn how to establish probable cause in your reports. Probable cause can be defined as "reasonable grounds for making a search or pressing a charge" or "a reasonable belief that a person has committed a crime." It's a little—OK, a lot—more complicated than that, but they'll drill it into your head in the academy.

You never want the academy to be the first time you're seeing something, because if it is, you're behind the power curve. Do yourself a favor; Google "police report writing," and get a little practice in. That way, when you get to this lesson plan in the academy, you already have basic practical knowledge.

TIPS:

- Cover the basics of every scene (who, what, when, where, why).

- Get as much contact/ identifying information as possible for your report (phone numbers, emails, social media, addresses, family contacts, etc.).

- Proofread your reports before submitting them. Remember these reports may be read in a courtroom one day.

- Avoid shorthand and cop terminology. Fully spell out every word, unless you annotate otherwise at the beginning of your report. For example, "I then made contact with the victim, identified as Marilyn (who will hereafter only be referred to as 'the victim')."

- Remember, don't make up information, and don't assume that information is or will be inferred. Detail everything that happened, and leave it at that.

<u>Patrol Procedures</u>

Also known as the way the department regulates how you do your job. **Pro tip:** Understand that there is the law, and then there is the law your department will set out in the form of policy, which will always be more restrictive. This is the more restrictive departmental policy, the standard operating procedures (SOPs) of your future agency. They will cover everything from show-up, vehicle/personnel equipment allowed on patrol to uniform regulations, lunch breaks, vehicle pursuits, and when to call in specialized units.

Be sure to pay attention, and don't let however long this block of instruction is in your academy be the only time you look at your departmental policies. These are procedures that, if you violate them too often or if a single offense is severe enough, can and will get you fired. When I went through the academy, an instructor told my class that, as a rookie, he would read one departmental policy a day, every day. I tried that, and it sucked, so I stopped. But I do make it my business to read one policy on each day that I go to work, before I hit the streets. The benefits and payoffs have been amazing. When I was a one-year officer, senior officers would often check with me on policy while on calls to make sure we hit all the check boxes. Why? Policy changes often, especially in bigger departments. What was OK a few months ago may be a no-no now. Be a source of information for your classmates and your shift, once you hit the streets, and you'll go far.

In the academy, you should be reading one policy every single day, regardless whether it's your off day or not. It will put you miles ahead of your classmates and pay major dividends when you hit the streets on FTO.

TIPS:

- **Keep in mind that ignorance isn't bliss when it comes to understanding what you can and can't do. If you don't understand a policy, then ask your instructor. If you're on the streets, ask a senior officer or a supervisor.**

Investigations

Everything they teach you in the academy is important, but knowing how to properly investigate when on scene is critical. You absolutely need to have the ability to show up on scene, often after the fact, take in all the available information and evidence, and draft a logical conclusion. It's around 90 percent of our job; from crashes to homicides, you will be asked to investigate on a daily basis.

I'm going to be real with you; there isn't really any hocus pocus here, there isn't a secret trick to it. The only prerequisite is common sense and good judgment. Your academy may teach different methods of interviewing suspects and may require different forms for various calls. That's all neither here nor there, and you will catch on quickly.

I've found that two things really help with becoming great at investigations. Know the law and know your department's policies and procedures. I'll say it again, and any cop with time on the streets will say it as well, scenes can get CRAZY! You'll have a million and one things running through your head, such as the safety of everyone on scene, medical aid, and more. If you're also trying to figure out what you should be doing next or what charge you have, you won't be in the moment, and you'll miss critical pieces of information. Knowledge is confidence on the streets; when you know what to do and how to do it, you can focus on conducting a thorough investigation.

This translates directly to your success in the academy, specifically when you start conducting scenarios, during which your instructors will be evaluating how you investigate, as well as your understanding and knowledge of the law and departmental policy. You see how it's all starting to fit together?

<u>TIPS:</u>

- The two biggest mistakes cadets and rookies make when conducting an investigation, both in mock scenarios and on the streets, are rushing through investigations and not asking enough detailed questions.
- Once a scene is safe, slow everything down, and be inquisitive. It's only rarely that rushing through an initial investigation is mission critical. More likely, a good, thorough investigation will help detectives and prosecutors down the line make a solid case.
- Don't be afraid to ask people to repeat information. People have varying speech patterns and accents, and having someone repeat information to be sure you documented it right can go a long way toward catching mistakes or misunderstandings.

<u>Traffic Accident Investigations</u>

Probably one of the most dangerous things a cop can do is work a crash. Just Google the statistics, or better yet, ask your academy instructor to view any of the hundreds of videos of officers getting creamed by vehicles on crash scenes. It's a dangerous part of the job, especially on high-speed roadways.

During this block of instruction, you'll learn how to position your patrol vehicle, process the crash scene, provide emergency medical treatment, call for EMS and fire, direct traffic, and document your final findings. Crashes are often multi-pronged evolutions that can require many resources and a lot of time. Be sure to pay close attention during this block, and ALWAYS WEAR YOUR REFLECTIVE SAFETY VEST.

<u>TIPS:</u>

- Cant your wheels outward once parked on scene. This way, if your car is struck while you are out processing the scene, your vehicle won't ram into you or anyone else still at the crash site.
- It's best to do most of your crash work (e.g., writing tickets, exchanging driver information) out of your car and away from any line of traffic.
- If you are working in your car on the scene of a crash, wear your seatbelt.
- Remember to not get sucked into your ticket writer, meaning always check your surroundings, keeping an eye out for hazards and people. A good, basic rule of thumb is to bring whatever you're working on up to eye level so that you can use your peripheral vision to watch for threats and danger.

<u>Emergency Vehicle Operations (EVOC)</u>

If you're originally from a city that has great public transportation, and you've never really had a reason to drive, you're going to struggle. You need to have been driving long before the academy starts and definitely long before you get to this block of instruction. Like investigations, everything you learn is important in the academy, but safely operating your patrol vehicle is a critical function. It will be how you get to calls, transport prisoners, eat your lunch; it's your home away from home, and you need to be able to handle that puppy.

Seriously, you need to be driving a lot before you get to this block of instruction. It's no secret how challenging many of these academy driving courses are. Look for some on YouTube; many departments are more than proud of the fact that their driving course is insane. The techniques they show you have real-life applications, specifically in pursuits.

Pursuits are the thing almost everyone thinks of when they say the words "police officer." The truth is, they're fun but extremely dangerous, especially for civilians and pedestrians. You need to not only be cognizant of your vehicle and driving capabilities but also those of the suspect vehicle and the innocent bystanders you're sharing the road with. Our primary duty is to protect the public . . . but I'm rambling; they'll cover that in more detail for you in the academy.

Pro Tip: Get as many reps in of driving and operating your car in reverse before the academy; it'll pay off big time.

<u>TIPS:</u>

- **Be sure to adjust the seat, mirrors, and steering controls if your academy has you hot-swapping patrol units during training. Nothing is worse than doing your final EVOC evaluation and being crunched up against the steering wheel, not being able to see out the mirrors for a reverse course, or being too far from the brakes.**

Basic First Aid/CPR

On patrol, you will often be the first person on scene, arriving before fire and EMS. In situations where emergency medical intervention is required, an officer will be expected to assess and help remedy the situation. Gunshot victims, choking babies, and people injured in car accidents will all be depending on you to give that initial first aid.

Some of the skills you may learn will be CPR, and basic life support (BLS). Some agencies may even train you in advanced life support (ALS). You'll also learn how to use various tourniquets, treat sucking chest wounds, splint bone breaks, and pack gauze.

Do yourself a favor and sign up for a community CPR class at your local YMCA or other community nonprofit and get some exposure. Hands-on practice is the best, though if you are in a pinch, looking at online videos and training resources is the next best thing.

<u>TIPS:</u>

- **While having a medical kit in your patrol kit is a great idea, be sure to make at least one tourniquet a part of your on-person carry. Keep it either on your duty belt or in a uniform pocket. Things happen away from patrol vehicles, and you may not have the time or ability to get back to your bag.**
- **Medical training, like firearms and defensive tactics, is a diminishing skill; be sure to keep up on your medical treatment skills.**

Computers/Information Systems

Policing is stepping into the modern era; all across the nation, departments are adopting new systems and technology to help officers do their jobs better. Usually, the technology is more of a headache than its worth, but some hotshot salesman has sold the department brass on the idea, so now you have it.

Today, policing is reliant on a lot of tech gadgets. These include the mobile data terminal (MDT), or computer, in your car, where you can view and assign to calls, message dispatch and other units, look up criminal history reports, and a whole host of other things. There is also the new E-ticket writing systems with the ability to take pictures, issue tickets, scan vehicles and IDs, and instantly send them off. In addition, there is automated license plate recognition (ALPR) and the StarChase systems used to automatically scan for stolen vehicles and remotely track suspects who flee custody in cars. It's a reality of the profession, and you'll be expected to adapt.

Honestly, most cadets of the current generation won't have an issue adapting and adopting the new technology. If you grew up with computers, gaming systems, and advanced cell phones, you'll be fine; besides, the tech in most patrol cars isn't even close to being on par with civilian capabilities. However, if you're older and never really took to all the new advancements in technology, you'll probably want to take a basic computer familiarity course online or in person.

Firearms/Defensive Tactics/Use of Force

<u>Defensive Tactics</u>

This is my personal favorite, though I'm admittedly a tad biased on the subject, being a defensive tactics (DT) instructor myself. If you've read our other book *Applicant to Police Cadet* or followed our blog at CadetRookieCop.com, you'll know it's a passionate topic for me. DT saves lives, plain and simple. I'll leave it at this: If you're a cop, and you don't train in some sort of functional martial art, it's going to bite you in the rear one day. And if you're a cadet coming into the academy having never been in a scrap, or trained, you're going to have a really long week and perform very poorly.

I'm extremely judgmental when it comes to other departments' DT programs or lack thereof. Yes, there are still some small departments out there who don't have one or that are using archaic practices. That aside, a good DT program will have you spar and train not only against your classmates but against the instructors as well. No one there will be trying to permanently injure you, but you will be punched in the body and the face repeatedly. No different than what a crook would do to you on the street when you try to arrest them and they don't feel like wearing your fancy bracelets.

"Yeah, well, I used to box, so I'll be fine." I hear it all the time.

Maybe you did, maybe you do, maybe you're Pacquiao's little brother or sister and a Golden Gloves champ—that's phenomenal! But a little word to the wise from an actual police academy DT instructor: TRAIN FOR THE GROUND! Jujitsu, wrestling, Sambo, or judo.

Have you ever heard of the UFC? I'm sure you have; it's the premier mixed martial arts organization in the world. You know who else has probably heard of it? The drug dealer on the corner, the violent husband who abuses his wife, and a whole host of unsavory characters; just so you know, the turds of our society also have access to television.

Have you ever watched a fight? Or seen highlights? You think criminals haven't? You think the drug dealer on the corner doesn't know what ground and pound is? Do you know what it is? Can you stop it from happening to you when you're less than arm's reach distance and you are attempting to hand-cuff your suspect? You probably want to. . . .

Sorry.

The academy instructor in me is coming out. Let me end the section with this: 90 percent of all conflicts end in some sort of grappling exchange. If you look at handcuffing, you're already in a grappling situation if and when things go south. Just take my advice and sign up for a month of jujitsu practice at your local gym; you'll thank me later.

<u>TIPS:</u>

- **Number one rule: If you pull a tool from your duty belt (Taser, oleoresin capsicum [OC] spray, ASP), make sure you are willing to use it and not just trying to intimidate. Know that you have the legal authority to apply the force you're about to apply.**

Firearm Skills and Tactics

This is that one area of the job you hope to never have to use, but you want the skills sharp and ready just in case your number gets called. We never know when that is, so you need to treat your firearms training as if you're going to get in a shooting your first day on FTO because you might. An instructor of mine said something profound to me when I was going through the academy: "No matter what call you go to, there will always be at least one gun on scene . . . yours." You want to know how to use and protect the most important tool on your duty belt.

Most academies have their own unique techniques and training methods as it pertains to firearms and tactics. If you're coming in with a wide array of firearms training and experience, then keep it to yourself and apply the techniques being taught. Don't be that guy who tries to show off; nobody likes that guy, and you'll get checked. For those of you who have never held a gun, I suggest going to a gun range and taking a basic pistol familiarity course. I have seen many cadets struggle during this block of instruction, often needing extensive remedial training, and sometimes getting cut from the program for unsatisfactory performance. You don't want that added stress on top of everything else you'll be expected to do while in the academy.

TIPS:

- **Remember: Treat, Never, Keep, Keep.**
- **Once the academy has trained you on their method of shooting, practice, practice, practice. You should dry fire your gun at least five times more than you shoot it live. Practice draws from your holster, reloads, and activating your weapon light.**

Use of Force

This will be the career-saving block of instruction for you in the academy. What you'll learn during this block of instruction will be when and to what severity you, as an officer, can react in certain situations. One of the cornerstones of our profession is understanding and implementing the use of force. Anytime you are required to use force on someone, it must be justified and reasonable. I can't stress enough how important this will be to not only your career but your livelihood as well. If you beat up a crook, or worse yet, shoot someone, you'd better be damned sure you followed the use of force policies and procedures of your department. If not, getting fired will probably be the least of your worries, as you could be looking at criminal charges and lawsuits.

There isn't too much for me to get into here. When you get this material in the academy, commit it to memory until it makes sense.

<u>TIPS:</u>

- Two things trip up police officers regarding use of force, and both are avoidable.
- First, officers hesitate. Hesitation can come from many things, but often it's because young officers aren't sure of what they're allowed to do in certain situations. They're afraid to overreact, so they underreact, which can lead to dangerous situations.
- The second issue is on the complete opposite end of the spectrum and is what makes the news—officers overreacting to situations and going far beyond what the situation dictates.
- Use of force and your training in firearms and defensive tactics are heavily intertwined. You need to not only be aware of the situation and where within the use of force you're currently operating but also be extremely secure and confident in your training and abilities. This actually helps to ensure the safety of everyone on scene, bad guys and officers alike.

Nonlethal Weapons

Oh, yay. Man, I don't know what sick individuals came up with some of the less than lethal options on our duty belts, but you'll get to know each one of them intimately. Jokes aside, when you cover these in the academy, it will be to gain familiarity with and confidence in the tools on your belt. You'll need to be able to testify in court to the device's effectiveness and effects on the body, and the only way to do this is with practical application.

The Taser

It is often yellow, sometimes black, and always on the opposite side of your firearm. Yes, you'll be Tased. Some Academies use gator clips that attach to your clothing, others just shoot you with an actual pronged cartridge. Personally, for me, it sucked a lot. But it's only a five-second ride, the effects of which quickly wear off after about ten or twenty minutes. Just as a heads-up, some academies may have you drive stun your own leg first to get you in the right frame of mind. Be prepared for that possibility. Hydrate and eat well the morning of this exercise; the stress the exposure puts on your body can take a lot out of you.

OC Spray

This is every academy instructor's favorite day. At least it is for me every time I see cadets get their OC exposure. You may be that fraction of a percent who is unaffected by OC spray; I know I was hoping for it. But the reality is you probably aren't. It burns—a lot. The best description I can give you is it's like the devil pissing in your eyes. It was literally the worst pain I have ever felt in my eyeballs to date. The effects can last up to four to six hours, depending on your sensitivity to the mixture. A word of advice: Don't watch any videos, and don't ask for horror stories; they will only make you more anxious. Just go in knowing it's something you have to do to get one step closer to graduation. **Pro Tip**: Nothing really works to neutralize the effects, at least that I've seen personally. Also, when you get home, wash your head separately in the shower to prevent the reflash from washing down to your more sensitive areas.

ASP/PR-24

This is also known as your police baton. Most academies will have this block of instruction to train you in one or two of these tools. To my knowledge, the only form of practical application with these consists of just hitting pads, not your fellow classmates.

Wellness/Self-Improvement

Ethics

I feel this will be pretty self-explanatory. This may last a day or even a week, depending on your academy's training curriculum, during which you'll cover things like honesty, integrity, and public trust. You will also be provided with tools and information to help you in areas such as

- **the language of ethics and professionalism;**
- **identifying ethical dilemmas and pitfalls;**
- **ethical decision-making;**
- **personal character in professional life;**
- **understanding the role of personal moral development, integrity, and character; and**
- **recognizing the consequences of both ethical and unethical behavior.**

You may be shown some examples of dirty cops and asked how these incidents affect the public perception of the law enforcement profession. It goes without saying that being ethical goes hand-in-hand with the job. Hence the long and excruciating background check into your personal life during the hiring process. Remember, everyone will make mistakes in this career; just own up to them, and more often than not, they can be forgiven. But if you lie, there is nothing anyone can do for you, and you can kiss your job goodbye.

<u>Health and Fitness</u>

As you read this, you may feel it doesn't apply to you. You may be a super-fit former college athlete or marathon runner who loves to eat right and work out twice a day. This isn't for you, and this instruction in the academy won't be for you, either. It's for the regular people, people who busted their tail to get in shape for the academy but plan on slacking off once they graduate. Be careful; it can be a slippery slope.

During this instructional block, you'll hear a lot about how unhealthy we are as a profession and most don't live to enjoy their retirement. It's all pretty true, late nights and odd shifts drive officers to go after what's open, and it isn't the smoothie store, let me tell ya. The academy will give you information and tips to stay healthy. It's one of those things that sneaks up on you over time, so maybe you take some of it to heart; maybe you don't.

Just keep in mind that being a fat cop is a safety risk, not only to yourself but to your partners on the patrol as well. No one is saying you have to be *Baywatch* ready, but be in good enough shape to win the fight and go home safe.

Communications

This will literally be how to talk to people. As silly as that may sound, you may find your communication skills to be lacking for your soon-to-be new profession. As a police officer, you can't talk to people the same way you would as a civilian. You'll need to be able to establish control of hectic scenes, calm raging suspects, and console sexual assault victims. The academy will look to give you some tools for improving your communications in the areas of

- **professionalism;**
- **communication theory; and**
- **tactics.**

You'll learn that situations on scene always go better when you can generate voluntary compliance, cooperation, and collaboration.

Professionalism

Much like communications, this block of instruction will be teaching you how to act as an officer of the law. It's important to understand, and should go without saying, that the way you carry and present yourself on and off duty will need to change, although given that you made it through the hiring process, hopefully not too drastically. Academies may focus on different aspects, but you can expect to cover topics such as

- **understanding that policing is a high-visibility profession and that you're always being watched or recorded;**
- **understanding that you'll have to make quick decisions;**
- **that you'll be held to a higher ethical standard than the public; and**
- **how your badge is a symbol of the public trust.**

There is a reason not just anyone can be a police officer.

<u>Stress Management</u>

Stress is also known as the cop killer, a.k.a. the marriage killer, a.k.a. the career killer. Stress will be an inescapable part of the job. I'm not a stress expert or a counselor, and I won't pretend to be. I do, however, serve as a peer support officer for my department. Through that training, I have gained a greater appreciation for the effects stress can have on officer's lives and the lives of their loved ones.

In the academy, this will probably sound like something that happens to other people and won't happen to you. That's because, in the academy, everything is safe. Out on the streets, when things get real, that repeated exposure can do some long-term damage. Take the information to heart, and when you graduate, if you find yourself or a shift mate acting out of character, get professional help.

Legal Studies

<u>Criminal and Constitutional Law</u>

This is the glue that's holds everything together and gives you your authority as an officer. Academically, this will be some of the most challenging tests you've ever taken. Often, the passing grade requirement is 80 percent or more. You need to have your studying methods down pat, take lots of notes, and fight the urge to fall asleep. You'll learn offenses, offense levels, punishments, culpable mental states, and probable cause. It will be a lot of information, akin to sucking water from a fire hose on full blast. Many cadets fall out academically during these weeks. Don't let it be you.

<u>Traffic Law</u>

My lowest scoring test in the academy was in transportation code (traffic law), and I'd studied. There are so many nuances in traffic law; everything from how many lights certain vehicles must have to how far the lights must be visible with the naked eye, to parking distances from stop signs and fire hydrants. I can't speak for everywhere else, but in Texas, traffic law is about three or four times thicker than criminal law. So I'll let that sink in for a minute.

The same advice applies here as with criminal law—take good notes and study, study, study.

That is about everything you can expect to cover during your time in the academy. Each academy is different. Some may focus on more detailed coursework for various topics. You may also experience regional training, such as wilderness survival, if your department operates in remote areas. These types of unique outliers are few and far between and are often expressed to you well in advance.

CHAPTER 2

Pre-Academy Preparation

Introduction

By this point, you know what the basic learning points are for the academy. But honestly, that's not really why you're here, right? You want to know how to get an award. The name of this book is *Graduating with Honors* after all, and you haven't seen honoring yet, am I right? We're getting there! Had to ease some of the fears that come with the unknown first, and get you in the right headspace.

Now that you hopefully understand just how important the academy is, we can begin to break down how to stand out from the pack. Now, let me be clear; some of these skills can't be acquired with just hard work and a can-do attitude. That's why I suggested reading our previous book *Applicant to Police Cadet* because preparation needs to begin as soon as you make up your mind that you truly want to be a cop. But by now, you're already in or nearing the end of your application process, so your skills are your skills, for the most part. Nothing beats an ironclad will to succeed; I'll tell you that much. And with that, you can overcome any deficiency in skill to surpass those around you.

As we move forward, I'm going to be dropping a lot of little nuggets of information. Some may seem out of your league, and they may be; others may make you feel uncomfortable, and that's good! You need to make it so you're comfortable being uncomfortable. The academy, if you invest the time and energy, should be one of the hardest things you've ever done in your life, the first notch on a list of monumental achievements you are destined to accomplish throughout your career. It's important to be realistic as you go through the sections of material and understand there are people out there well beyond your level, especially in the skill areas. What do I mean by that? Well, let's just say you don't stand the best shot of winning the firearms award over the guy who shoots at national competitions; also don't expect to get the fitness award over a SEAL or a sponsored marathon runner; you know, common sense stuff.

Even after taking to heart everything you will read from here on out, there will always be an intangible factor, and that's **LUCK**. You have to be a little lucky to rake in the goods at graduation. Take me, for example, dual expert marksman in the military with pistol and rifle; black belt in judo; in exceptional shape, scoring in the ninetieth percentile in my physical testing; and tested for E-6 within four years of being in the military (my veterans know what kind of work that means). With all that going on, you couldn't have told me I wasn't going to clean house in the academy. I was like, "I'm literally going to get every single award there is," and that was my goal! But guess what? Luck was not on my side; my class was full of monsters, true specimens of every skill and trade. I thought I was smart, but I had classmates scoring ninety-sevens on every test, while I hovered around a ninety average. I thought I was in shape; one of my classmates was a professional runner (actually got paid to run), he had something like a seven minute and change mile and a half. I thought I could shoot; well, one of my classmates was an ex-Special Forces and could shoot the target before I even drew my weapon. They all thought they could fight; until they came up against me (grinning widely). Yep, even with all my skills, I only managed to graduate with one award, the coveted Defensive Tactics Superiority Award. Why? The luck of the draw; I had a stacked class full of extremely talented and gifted individuals.

So as you prepare and execute your game plan, keep in mind that sometimes your best isn't **the** best, and you need to be OK with that.

Establish Leadership Early On

Believe it or not, the academy is primarily all about your class coming to together as a team. The longer you and your classmates try to hold on to your individuality, the longer and harder your academy days will be. Teamwork makes the dream work, baby! Seriously though, your class will need to rely on each other not only to graduate but on the streets as well.

This is where the first phase of your leadership comes into play.

Every academy I know of will have some sort of orientation before the actual start date. Family members may be invited, and you'll meet some of your initial instructors. This is where you will also see your fellow cadets for the first time. Remember what I said, right? Your reputation begins Day 1; orientation is your day one, and you need to establish yourself as a leadership presence.

You can do this in one of two ways (of course, other variations apply):

1. **If the instructor staff has everyone introduce themselves one at a time, then when it is your**

> turn, say your pleasantries and end with "At the conclusion of this orientation, I would like to meet with all of my future classmates in (pick a location—parking lot, hallway, etc.) so we can all exchange contact information."

2. If you don't have a chance to introduce yourself, then at the end of the orientation, if there is an opportunity to ask a question, stand up and make the same declaration. If that is also not an option, then once the orientation is over, stand up and announce the same statement.

The thought of doing something like this may make you nervous, but guess what? Everyone else is as well and will be thankful you took the stand. Additionally, right there in front of academy staff and family, you are making a huge statement of leadership and accountability.

See, once you get that invitation to the academy, there will be a whole host of other requirements you'll need to have accomplished before you show up the first day. Everything from paperwork to uniforms, IDs, and books, and it'll all be at various locations spread across the area. Having everyone's contact information will allow you to ensure your classmates are where they need to be when they need to be there. It will also be a great resource to have on Day 1 of the academy doing pre-show-up equipment checks.

When you meet with your classmates after orientation, get the following information written down:

- **Full name**
- **Cell phone number**
- **Facebook page (you'll understand why in a bit)**
- **Email**

If you're motivated, you can take all of that information, make an Excel or Word document, and blast it out to everyone's email. That may be easy to do for some people. Another just as effective way would be to keep everyone there until each person has had a chance to write down their info, then place the paper in the middle so everyone can enter each person's info into their cellphones themselves. Just do what feels best to you.

This step is **critical** to starting off your academy on the right foot.

What if someone speaks up before I get the chance to give my spiel?

Then you need to roger up and announce you'll be second in command and assist in the efforts of getting your classmates connected to one another. You absolutely need to be involved in this process no matter what.

Why Facebook?

For my class, we created a Facebook page to easily send out important class info and coordinate workout and study groups. It worked wonders, and often, notes that were missed were posted, along with useful tips and meet-up information.

Meet Up Often

You guys are going to be stuck together for months and eventually be each other's backup on the streets; you're going to want to start getting to know each other. This is not just for fun but also to find out each other's backgrounds and experience, strengths and weaknesses. Needless to say, you need to be the one pushing for and organizing these class meet-ups. Not everything you do needs to be known or seen by your academy instructors to count. You're building habits and a track record with your class as someone who cares about not only their own success but also the success of the whole team.

Form Workout Groups

Again, we are in the pre-academy stage still, so a quick heads-up. You're going to be working out a lot while you're in the academy, more than most people will or ever have in their lives. Some of your classmates may be struggling with keeping to a scheduled workout routine; you may be struggling to keep a set workout routine. In either case, accountability partners can make a world of difference. Also, I've always found it easier to work out harder when I'm around people; something about it always makes me want to push myself that much more. Running for long distances is also better in groups. It's like a proven science or something, and trust me, you'll need to be doing a lot of running.

Your class will only be as strong as your weakest link. If you're fit and you think that by shining on your classmates, outperforming everyone and making them look bad it will help you get an award, you are sadly mistaken. Being in shape is great—seriously, it is—but helping your team increase its overall fitness level is even better.

The fitness groups you create now can and should continue throughout the academy on your days off to help ensure everyone is within standards and can meet the fitness requirements.

<u>Form Study Groups</u>

It all comes back to accountability partners. Hands down, the number one thing that gets most cadets cut from the academy is academics. The academic standards of the academy are rigorous and unforgiving. When I went through, we had a test every Monday (including the first Monday, which was the first day of the academy). You had to score at least a seventy, but a seventy was considered substandard, and you would be required to write a memo. If you had an average grade in the seventies over two semesters, you would be fired in the third. To actually pass, you had to score an eighty or higher on each test. You were only allowed to fail three tests over the entire eight months of the academy. If you failed the test on Monday, you had a retake on Wednesday. If you failed the retake, you were terminated on the spot. Over the course of my academy, I saw no less than twenty classmates get the boot for poor academics.

Creating study groups will help you not only if you're a weak studier but also if you're a strong one. If you have your studying methods down, then helping fellow classmates get the material will allow you the opportunity to get a deeper understanding, benefitting you and the team.

Just like with the workout groups, this is something that you can set up and organize before the academy and utilize on a daily or weekly basis while the academy is in session.

The Cadet Manual

You want to really stand out from the rest of your classmates on Day 1 of the academy? Then know your cadet manual inside and out, like the back of your hand. The academy is all about attention to detail. Those details will be spelled out for you in the cadet manual, literally every single one. Knowing it and being confident in your understanding of the material will allow you to take charge on Day 1 of the academy, ensuring your class is set up for success. The cadet manual will cover everything from chain of command (know that) to 10-codes (know those, too), fallen officers (God help you if you don't know that one), uniform expectations, values of the department, cadet conduct expectations, and a whole host of other things. You and your class will be expected to know everything in that manual and execute it to the letter. Smoke sessions, outside of Day 1, are never scheduled; they're earned. Remember that.

Being able to answer questions from academy staff will go a long way, especially on Day 1. You want to be the one your classmates come to when they have a question about cadet policy. Lead by example, following the rules and guidelines set forth in the cadet manual, and you'll always be squared away.

Watch Videos on the Academy

Watch videos of actual police academies, not just yours, but other ones as well. Begin indoctrinating yourself into the mind-set of what will be required of you. This will also help with visualization. You want to be able to see yourself in the video; visualize yourself accomplishing the same tasks as the cadets in the video. Tell yourself every day, "If they could do it, so can I." You'll also be able to pick up on mistakes past cadets have made, ensuring you don't make the same ones. Preparing the mind is just as important as preparing the body. The academy plays a lot of mind games. These games are designed to weed the weak-minded and selfish individuals out of the class.

Eliminate All Distractions

The last thing I'll touch on for the pre-academy stage is the importance of a low- to no-stress environment at home, free from distractions. In the academy, your life is going to need to get real simple, real fast. Your day should look something like this:

- **Wake up (approximately one and a half to two hours before academy starts)**
- **Eat breakfast**
- **Stretch out the kinks from the previous day**
- **Get dressed**
- **Check and then double-check your equipment**
- **Drive to the academy**
- **Do academy stuff**
- **Leave**
- **Do study group**
- **Go home to study some more**
- **Eat dinner**
- **Go to sleep**
- **Repeat**

Seriously, it takes that kind of commitment, especially if you're trying to be an awardee. If you have a spouse or significant other, then you'll need to sit down and talk

everything out. They'll need to understand that the academy is going to require an astronomical amount of your time and energy. It will be up to you and your partner how you'll balance the time you need to study, work out, and train with the quality time they'll be expecting from you. No one said it'll be easy; I just said it'll be worth it in the end.
If you're into the whole PlayStation and Xbox thing, that will also have to stop. No time for games when you're trying to outperform everyone in your class. Plus, the time you'd spend playing video games could be time you spend with your family instead.

If you want to increase your chances of getting an award, then you have to be able to show that you not only know more than everyone in your class but that you can also apply that information in practice. The only way to get to that level is to study and practice in your off time.

CHAPTER 3

The First Day of the Academy

Introduction

Your first day of the academy—a monumental step toward the rest of your life. I can remember being excited, proud, and nervous all at the same time, along with an ever-growing feeling of dread and despair. But we'll touch on that later! So what is the first day like? Well, if your academy is worth its salt, it will forever stand out in your memory as one of the hardest days of your life. The mind games on Day 1 are on a whole other level, as well as the physical demands put on your body. Here is a little snippet of my first day in the academy; then we'll touch on how to master your first day.

Morning Inspections

Now, this was an expected event. I mean, we all knew it was coming, and yet we did so poorly (shaking my head). Basically, it went like this: As the start date for the academy neared, emails were sent out. Some were for picking up equipment; others were for taking pictures and ordering uniforms. One of these emails in particular stated that cadets would be expected to read, study, and regurgitate upon extreme interrogation the information given in the cadet handbook. This information consisted of chain of command, 10-codes, sectors, dos and don'ts for cadet behavior, and the history of fallen officers within the department. A lot of information, sure, but nothing terribly difficult.

Or so I thought; and boy, did I think wrong.

As we all went through the gauntlet, my classmates bombed each question repeatedly. With each incorrectly answered question, the dread and despair grew and grew until I was sure that we were going to get the business right there on the spot. The anticipation that at any moment we would be forced to repent for our ignorance kept me on edge. But to my surprise, our ICs only yelled. All things considered, it was quite moderate. I began to relax a little.

Maybe things wouldn't be as bad as I had worked them up to be in my mind.

Death by PowerPoint

We were then all ushered into the classroom, where I experienced a hell like no other. Death by PowerPoint. It's real, it sucks, and the pain transcends the mental realm. The sheer boredom and monotony of the PowerPoint presentations manifested themselves as a physical pain within my body, for which the only relief was sleep. Did I fall victim to the sweet embrace of sleep? Yes, yes I did. I honestly believe that at some point, we all did, instructor included. Each time I would leave this world to join the dream realm, I would snap awake, fear that I had been spotted by an IC racking my body. But each time, the ICs remained silent and in their seats at the back of the classroom. I relaxed a bit more.

Maybe they understood that the PowerPoints sucked? I thought, "This won't be so bad after all; I'm liking the academy so far."

Death by Paperwork

Have you ever written so much that your hand cramped? Have you ever signed your name so much that you forgot how to sign your name? Again, it's real, and it sucks. There was a litany of paperwork, forms, documents, benefits, legal work, departmental hoopla—it seemed it would never end. Something I noticed during the process was that every single document was extremely important. I found it odd because my screw-ups were at an all-time low by that time, and I marveled at the sheer audacity of it all. Here I was, half-insane from the PowerPoint barrage, reading and signing legally binding documents that determined pay, benefits, and other important things. But still no smoke sessions, no intense physical torment. Things were looking up.

True Death

Have you ever seen *True Blood* on HBO? My wife put me on to it some years back. It's a vampire chick flick kind of show, but it grows on you. Anyway, one thing the vampires in the show are most in fear of is the True Death, a death they cannot come back from. This is essentially what I went through for damned near three hours as my body experienced a level of exhaustion I had not felt up to that point in my life and that I haven't felt since.

Let me explain.

At that point in the day, all of the cadets were thoroughly mentally drained but relatively well off overall. Lunch was a peaceful time as we grazed, unmolested by the ICs. The day was almost over; I think we had about an hour and a half or so before we would be cut loose. The general feeling among my classmates was, "Hey, we must've impressed the ICs enough that they aren't going to smoke us or anything." Plus, we figured if they did, we wouldn't be outside for too long since the workday was pretty much over.

The problem, we soon learned, was twofold. First, we had not impressed the ICs with our conduct during the day, not even a little bit. Second, time was a barrier that they were willing and able to overcome, with extreme prejudice.

One minute, we were sitting in the classroom ready to be released, and the next, we were being ordered outside to the herald of curses and screams. Waiting for us outside was a police showing so large, I was sure the streets weren't being adequately manned. Yelling, screaming, exercise, pain, exercise, cursing, screaming. It went like that for a while—about an hour and a half while. During the whole thing, I managed to glance at my watch and found solace in the fact that 4:00 p.m. was five minutes away. Soon, it would all be over. My strength renewed, I pushed through the pain, light firmly in view at the end of the proverbial tunnel.

They lined us up a bit past 4:00 p.m., nothing excessive, say 4:15. The yelling continued along with insults and the rest. But a conclusion to the madness was at hand. Finally, the words "Get out of my sight!" were given. The herd, meaning us cadets, made its way to safety. As we arrived at the door to the classrooms to retrieve our belongings and flee, we discovered a problem. The doors were locked, and none of us had the key. Horror began to set in among the crowd of cadets.

Standing there so close to salvation, I came to a cold realization—we weren't done. They weren't letting us go home. "Y'all still outside?! Must want some more! Line it back up!" That's all I remember before my soul left my body, and I entered into a physical hell. There were fire department water hoses, a mountain run, and I believe a unicorn, though I cannot be sure what was real and what was the dehydration. We eventually went home that day at 5:30 p.m., dripping wet, exhausted, confused, and half-conscious.

Something you never forget is your first day at the academy.

That was a little taste of my first day at the academy, and if you ask any cop about their first day, it'll bring an instant smile to their face. It's something we all have to go through, but you never go through it alone. It's the foundation that will serve as the rest of your career, something you and your classmates can always look back on fondly. Embrace the suck, as my IC used to say, embrace the suck!

Day 1 of the Academy

If you've been paying attention up to this point, then you've realized by now that it isn't just enough for *you* to be squared away; your whole class needs to be squared away, or at least as many as humanly possible. There will always be a few duds in the group; I think it's an EEOA thing. But excluding them, the more of your class that you can get to be on point at Day 1, the better your day and the closer you'll be to earning yourself an award at graduation. Remember, no one expects you to be a full-fledged officer Day 1 of the academy. Instructors aren't even looking for those attributes during Day 1; instead, they're looking for leaders, people who show up squared away and jump at the opportunity to display effective leadership.

The operative word here is "effective," not just leadership. Being motivated and eager to lead your classmates is great, but doing so without having sharpened your leadership ability will only hurt you. One of the best ways to ensure the support of your classmates is through building a report. This is easily accomplished if you've followed the advice laid out earlier in the book. If you skimmed through, you should go back and dial in the information. You want to be the person cadets and instructors call on for positive reasons. All of Day 1 is a reestablishment of your reputation.

<u>Understanding Your First Day</u>

Expect to be confused: No matter how prepared you are, the first day of the academy will be designed to confuse you and throw you off your game. You'll be called (or ordered) to do things you've never had to do before. At this point, avoid volunteering for any leadership position because it's often extremely temporary and the focal point of much abuse.

Military bearing: This is where being a veteran will pay dividends, and you'll begin to separate yourself. Being in the band will also have given you these skills to some degree. You'll be ordered into formation almost immediately upon arrival for your first inspection. If you've never done anything like it before, don't worry; most people haven't. Work on a good poker face; the more confident and serious you look coupled with a crisp uniform or suit should buy you some leeway.

Being yelled at: Look, it's part of the process, so get used to being yelled at for making mistakes. It's going to happen—often, if not because of you, then because of your classmates. Instructors will be looking to establish discipline and efficiency the second you step on campus. Just roll with the blows, keep your face neutral, and your responses sharp and respectful.

Plan on being physically tortured: With exercise, calm down, even though at times you'll feel like it's actual abuse. Keep in mind that it's designed to weed out those who aren't prepared, either physically or mentally. It won't last forever.

***You need to understand that everything that goes on Day 1 is carefully orchestrated and designed to evaluate cadets on a myriad of different skills. Don't focus on what is happening; just focus on doing your best. If you slack off in the group physical training (PT) sessions, it'll be noticed, I promise you. Instructors can tell who isn't going all out. Always go all out.**

Mastering Day 1 of the Academy

Your reputation begins when? Day 1! So you need to bring it with everything you have starting Day 1.

- **The number one thing you need to ensure is that you are squared away. What does that mean, and what does it look like?**
  - **Uniform or suit is pressed, professionally, if you can afford it. Use a lint roller before you get in and after you get out of the car. Burn or cut off loose threads.**
  - **Hair and nails are within regulations and standards. Face clean-shaven, unless you're a rebel like me, then rock a cadet-approved mustache. But know that if you do, they'll check and recheck to make sure it's within regulations. However, it does help you stand out from the pack.**
  - **Boots or shoes are mirror polished. Yes, they're going to be scuffed like hell by the end of the day, but you want to show up casket ready.**
  - **KNOW YOUR CADET MANUAL! EVERY SINGLE PIECE OF IT!**

- Double- and triple-check that you have all of your materials and equipment before you leave the house.
- Show up early. Don't be late; please don't be late. Someone always will be, but just don't let it be you.
- If you see any officer, instructor or not, get out of their way and address them respectfully.

Those are the basics to ensure you have as positive an experience as is possible on your first day. Next, I'll give some tips for how to blow your instructors out of the water on your first day.

- **Already have your classmates, or as many as you can, functioning as a team. This is when all those group meetings pay off big time. At your meetings, have the veterans teach basic formation organization and practice basic facing movements.**
- **Have your whole class, or as many as you can, know their cadet manual. This is where the study groups you've organized will pay off.**
- **Have the whole class show up early and conduct your own pre-inspection. Your cadet manual**

should have the expected grooming and uniform standards. Get any glaring mistakes fixed before the instructors get a chance to call them out.

- **During your many PT vacations, finish among the front of the pack every time, and then go back to encourage and work out with the stragglers. You do this Day 1, and you'll be the talk of the break room, I promise you. Most of your classmates will finish their run, or whatever the evolution is, and then take their well-deserved break. While they're doing that, you need to be running and working out with your classmates who fell behind. Then call on those classmates who've finished to come join them as well.**
- **Take on minor leadership rolls; pass out papers, help get water jugs, anything!**

These are the separating factors that will skyrocket your reputation as a cadet. You'll notice that your name will begin to be called by the instructors. Your classmates will also begin to nominate you for various leadership positions. You don't have to be the best leader out there; you just have to work harder than everyone else and take care of your classmates.

CHAPTER 4

The Weeks to Come

Keeping Your Foot on the Gas

Day 1 will become Day 2; Week 3 will become Week 9. You'll learn, and you'll grow. Amid all of the PT, academics, and skills, you need to always keep your eye on the end goal—graduating with honors. Your classmates' only goal will probably be simply to graduate, and so they'll always make sure they do just enough to achieve that. For you, graduation isn't enough, and the minimum isn't enough; you want to make sure you leave your mark and start your career off on the best foot possible. Consistency is the name of the game in the academy. You aren't always going to perform the best at every evolution, and you're not going to score the highest on every test, but you must remain consistent. The academy is a marathon, not a sprint; the pace you set on Day 1 needs to be something you can sustain over months. Nothing looks worse than starting off strong and then waning in the latter part of the academy.

Staying motivated will be a hard thing to do throughout the entire term of the academy. You may become jaded with underperforming classmates who cause you and your class to continually get punished. You may have a bad day and screw up; hell, you may have a bad week. Nobody will excel at everything in the academy; at least I haven't seen anyone do it. Remember when you mess up that everyone does at some point. Having a firm grasp on why you want to become a police officer in the first place will help you get through those tough times and push you when you feel like being lazy.

Another great thing to do if you find yourself in a constant state of being unmotivated is to hang with the top people in your class. These are the people who will be giving you your stiffest competition at graduation, so why not be around the best your class has to offer? Being around the best and brightest in your class does two things: one, it forces you to keep or increase your level of effort to match theirs, or risk being left behind; and two, it allows you to learn and pick up their successful habits. No matter how good you are at something or how well you're performing in the academy, there is always something that can be improved and new information that can be picked up.

The next piece of advice is to continue to perform all your pre-academy and Day 1 habits. You should still be organizing study groups, staying behind to help with remedial instruction, showing up early (ideally first), and being the last to leave. Ask permission to stay after classes one or two days a week to work out with the out-of-shape cadets in your class. The key to success for yourself is to help those around you succeed while maintaining the high standards of the academy. I guarantee you it won't be easy, but that's why so few cadets ever graduate with an award. You have to not only exceed standards but help those around you as well.

You want to be engaged in each one of your classes and instructional blocks. When instructors ask questions, be sure to always raise your hand and give an answer (a good answer). You should be doing this until the instructors say something like, "Anyone but (insert your name here)," or "(insert your name here) put your hand down; someone else give me an answer." The academy staff will begin to remember your name for positive reasons, and you'll often have many responsibilities placed on you. This all pays dividends over the course of the academy, especially if there are events or instructional blocks you are struggling with. Your track record as a leader and model cadet will carry you through those weak spots, and you'll often be given more leeway than other cadets who are doing only the minimum each day.

Getting Sick

It's a possibility that you may get sick. Being in close proximity to people who have varying standards of personal hygiene on a daily basis will always carry that risk. If you do get sick in the academy, then you'll need to conduct a self-assessment; do you have a fever, diarrhea, mucus, body aches? Most of the symptoms associated with being sick can be treated with over-the-counter medicine and a little perseverance. Only you know your body, so regardless of what anyone else says, if you can't push through, you can't push through. Your instructors may place you on light duty (LD) or send you home for a day or two. The latter happened to me while I was in the academy.

We were just coming off of our weekend, and I had gone out to eat that Sunday with my wife. Unbeknownst to me at the time, the establishment had less-than-ideal sanitation standards, and I got a stomach bug. Not just any stomach bug, mind you, but one that came with the big three: fever, vomiting, and diarrhea. I was up all night that night in the bathroom; I probably got all of thirty minutes of sleep. Despite all that, I still showed up to the academy the next day, sick and feverish, to take my Monday exam. I spent the whole beginning of the morning in the bathroom until the very last second before the test was about to begin. I then sat there, miserable, for forty minutes, throwing up in my mouth and swallowing it, while clenching my butt cheeks shut to avoid an accident while I took my test. The moment I completed the test, I rushed out of the testing room and into the nearest toilet. I tell you the story not to gross you out but to illustrate my personal level of dedication to the academy. I made my mind up that day that I wasn't going to go home unless they sent me home by force—which they eventually did, by the way.

My personal advice is that if you're sick, then push through it and continue to show up every day of academy training. But here's a full disclaimer: I am not a doctor, and you are an adult, so make the best decision for you and your body based on your symptoms. Be aware that if you miss too many days, it can reflect negatively on you, and missing too many critical training days can also result in your termination.

Getting Injured

With the physical demands that the academy places on your body, injury is always a lurking possibility. Taking proper care of your body during your free time can go a long way. Things like proper rest, stretching before and after the academy, and rest are habits that you should implement early on. Even so, I doubt there has ever been a cadet who has gone through the academy and stayed 100 percent healthy.

If there is one mistake many cadets make during the academy time and time again, it's confusing being hurt with being injured. You will get hurt in the academy; it's a given. Being punched in the face hurts. Accidently being hit with a baton hurts. Tripping and falling down during a group run also hurts. You may bleed, you may bruise, but YOU'RE OK! Don't ask to go LD, and don't ask for paperwork; just suck it up. Now, being injured is a completely different thing that no one likes to see. Broken bones, torn ligaments, concussions, heat strokes, severe allergic reactions to OC spray are all real, and all would constitute an injury, at least in my book. An injury means that your body cannot physically perform and is severely damaged. A sprained wrist doesn't count. Trust me on this, I have seen cadets lose everything by playing the injured game, thinking they were getting one over by missing out on PT sessions and other training evolutions, when really, they were just putting themselves in a deeper and deeper pit, to eventually be fired.

Alternatively, if you're truly injured, REPORT IT! Don't be that guy running around with a fractured rib for two months. It's admirable, but ultimately stupid. They won't make you sit out if you don't want to, but at least everyone on the staff will know what is going on with you. Again, you're an adult, or you will be when you go through the academy, so only you can make that call. Just use my opinion as a resource to help you better evaluate all of your options.

The Skill Weeks

The skills weeks may be called something else where you're going, but in the end, they're all the same. The Big Three, as I affectionately call them: firearms, driving, and defensive tactics. In the majority of academies across the nation, you'll be able to earn an award for each one of these skills. Some academies may average out your total score between the three and determine an award that way. As I stated earlier and in our previous book *From Applicant to Police Cadet*; skills are just that, skills. By definition, a skill is the ability to do something well, expertise. The last time I checked, you didn't become an expert in something over the course of a week in the academy unless you're some sort of super genius. I say this to highlight that the number one key to success in the academy is PREPARATION. If you don't know how to shoot going into the academy, the chances of you closing the skill gap to achieve a high level of proficiency in a week or two are slim to none. You'll pass, sure, but no one gives an award for just passing in the academy.

If you want to be in contention for a Big Three award, then you're going to have to put in the work beforehand. There's no secret there; if you want to be the top shot, you'll need to go to the range and shoot under instruction. If you want to be the top driver, then you'll need to do driving courses. And if you want to be the top fighter, then you'll need to train. For how long? I can't say; it depends on your aptitude and drive, but at a minimum, a solid sixty to ninety days.

So, what if you do all of that and you have some skills? You're golden, right? Wrong; the chances are extremely high that you'll be among at least a few who have the skills necessary to win the awards. So what will be the determining factors, the intangibles?

Humility is the first intangible. No one likes a cocky butthole. Being humble isn't something you learn overnight; it has to kind of just happen to you. But it will go a long way. When I was in the academy, the DT instructors asked us who had any martial arts experience. A few of my classmates raised their hands and spouted off their experience; I remained silent. My thought process was that I wanted to show them through the performance of the material that I had experience. How's the old saying go again? If you have to tell everyone how good you are, then you aren't as good as you think. If you're really that sweet, then your peers will talk of your prowess, and you'll never have to say a word.

Working hard is the second intangible, and it may seem like an obvious trait to have, but somehow it always gets lost in the mix. Just because you're a skilled marksmen, fighter, or driver doesn't mean you can just rest on your laurels until the finals come up. You need to be in the trenches with the rest of your classmates, doing the reps, doing the basics, and doing them better than everyone around you.

Speaking of classmates, that brings me to the final intangible factor, and that's helping your classmates succeed and meet minimum standards. This can be done by asking your skill instructors if it's OK for you to help your struggling class-mates during class, showing up to the remedial training after regular hours and assisting your classmates and instructor staff there. And if a remedial training doesn't exist, helping to create one. You can also offer free training to your peers in your off time to help them get better. These are all things I did while I was in the academy to earn my DT award, and it worked for me.

Skills, hard work, and selflessness will see you walking that graduation stage with honors; I guarantee it.

Character

This is the final section of this training resource and arguably the most important, your character. Look, being a cop is an A-type personality profession. I get it, but there are also such things as having humility, honor, integrity, and respect in this profession, not only for yourself and your classmates but for the staff and the community members you'll one day serve. Yeah, serve; it's an aspect of the policing profession that gets forgotten nowadays, that part about public service. I'll say this because I've seen it happen numerous times in the academy: Remember to have good character. Be honest; if you're struggling, never look for the easy way out. Don't cheat on tests, slack on PT exercises when no one is looking, or skip investigation steps to make them go by quicker because it will all come back to haunt you. It always does, and it is never worth the consequences. I knew a cadet in my class who seemingly had it all going for him. He was older and a retired military captain. The cadet staff were naturally drawn to his charismatic leadership ability, but he struggled academically. One day, a Monday, specifically, also known as test day, this star cadet got pulled out of class. His name was also stripped from the board of active cadets, and we would later find out that he had not only cheated on the test but had then lied about it to cadet staff when they questioned him. As a result, that individual can no longer apply for my department, and quite possibly nowhere in the state of Texas. He essentially blackballed himself from ever working as a law enforcement officer. You don't want that to be you, so always walk in your morals and make the right choices.

Remarks

These are all the tips and advice we could muster to help you master your academy. All of the knowledge here has been applied or observed personally. We know it works; you just have to apply yourself and remain consistent. Do that, and I know we'll see you on the streets soon, doing your part to keep your community safe. Good luck out there!

<u>Check out more phenomenal law enforcement resources at:</u>

CadetRookieCop.com

CadetRookieCop.com is quickly becoming the number one online educational resource for law enforcement professionals, law enforcement applicants, cadets, rookies, and the community members they serve.

OTHER EDUCATIONAL OFFERINGS

Available on Amazon

The Rookie Handbook: A Quick Reference Guide to Calls for Service

From Applicant to Police Cadet: How to Navigate the Police Hiring Process

Coming Soon

The Expert Witness

Be sure to Leave Us a Review on Amazon!!

www.ingramcontent.com/pod-product-compliance
Lightning Source LLC
Chambersburg PA
CBHW031143250726

48655CB00002B/804